RED OCEAN TRAPS

HARVARD BUSINESS REVIEW
CLASSICS

RED OCEAN TRAPS
The Mental Models That Undermine Market-Creating Strategies

W. Chan Kim and Renée Mauborgne

Harvard Business Review Press
Boston, Massachusetts

Copyright 2017 Harvard Business School Publishing Corporation
Originally published in *Harvard Business Review* in March 2015
Reprint #R1503D

Cataloging-in-Publication data is forthcoming.

ISBN: 978-1-63369-266-4
eISBN: 978-1-63369-267-1

The paper used in this publication meets the requirements of the American National Standard for Permanence of Paper for Publications and Documents in Libraries and Archives Z39.48-1992.

THE HARVARD BUSINESS REVIEW CLASSICS SERIES

Since 1922, *Harvard Business Review* has been a leading source of breakthrough ideas in management practice—many of which still speak to and influence us today. The HBR Classics series now offers you the opportunity to make these seminal pieces a part of your permanent management library. Each volume contains a groundbreaking idea that has shaped best practices and inspired countless managers around the world—and will change how you think about the business world today.

RED OCEAN TRAPS

In America, corporate performance has been deteriorating for decades. According to Deloitte's landmark study "The Shift Index," the aggregate return on assets of U.S. public companies has fallen below 1%, to about a quarter of its 1965 level. As market power has moved from companies to consumers, and global competition has intensified, managers in almost all industries have come to face steep performance challenges. To turn things around, they need to be more creative in developing and executing their competitive strategies. But long-term success will not be achieved through competitiveness alone. Increasingly, it will depend on the ability to generate new demand and create and capture new markets.

The payoffs of market creation are huge. Just compare the experiences of Apple and Microsoft. Over the past 15 years, Apple has made a series of successful market-creating moves, introducing the iPod, iTunes, the iPhone, the App Store, and the iPad. From the launch of the iPod in 2001 to the end of its 2014 fiscal year, Apple's market cap surged more than 75-fold as its sales and profits exploded. Over the same period,

Microsoft's market cap crept up by a mere 3% while its revenue went from nearly five times larger than Apple's to nearly half of Apple's. With close to 80% of profits coming from two old businesses—Windows and Office—and no compelling market-creating move, Microsoft has paid a steep price.

Of course, it's not that companies don't recognize the value of new market spaces. To the contrary, their leaders increasingly are committed to creating them and dedicate significant amounts of money to efforts to do so. But despite this, few companies seem to crack the code. What, exactly, is getting in their way?

In the decade since the publication of the first edition of our book, *Blue Ocean*

Strategy, we've had conversations with many managers involved in executing market-creating strategies. As they shared their successes and failures with us, we identified a common factor that seemed to consistently undermine their efforts: their mental models—ingrained assumptions and theories about the way the world works. Though mental models lie below people's cognitive awareness, they're so powerful a determinant of choices and behaviors that many neuroscientists think of them almost as automated algorithms that dictate how people respond to changes and events.

Mental models have their merits. In dangerous times, a robust mental model can help you quickly make decisions that are critical to survival. And we have no issue with the soundness of the mental models that we saw managers apply. They were grounded in knowledge acquired in classrooms and from years of business experience. They help managers respond better to competitive challenges. But our conversations suggest that the mental models managers rely on to negotiate existing market spaces also undermine their ability to create new markets.

In our research and discussions, we've encountered six especially salient assumptions built into managers' mental models. We have come to think of them as red ocean traps, because they effectively anchor managers in red oceans—crowded market spaces where companies engage in bloody competition for market share—and prevent them from entering blue oceans, previously unknown and uncontested market spaces with ample potential.

The first two traps stem from assumptions about marketing, in particular an emphasis on customer orientation and niches; the next two from economic lessons on technology innovation and creative destruction; and the final two from principles of competitive strategy that regard differentiation and low cost as mutually exclusive choices. In the following pages, we'll look at each trap in detail and see how it thwarts companies' attempts to create markets.

TRAP ONE: SEEING MARKET-CREATING STRATEGIES AS CUSTOMER-ORIENTED APPROACHES

Generating new demand is at the heart of market-creating strategies. It hinges on converting noncustomers into customers, as Salesforce.com did with its on-demand CRM software, which opened up a new market space by winning over small and midsize firms that had previously rejected CRM enterprise software.

The trouble is that managers, especially those in marketing, have been quite reasonably brought up to believe that the customer is king. It's all too easy for them to assume, therefore, that market-creating

strategies are customer led, which causes
them to reflexively stick to their focus
on existing customers and how to make
them happier.

This approach, however, is unlikely
to create new markets. To do that, an
organization needs to turn its focus
to noncustomers and why they refuse
to patronize an industry's offering.
Noncustomers, not customers, hold the
greatest insight into the points of pain and
intimidation that limit the boundary of an
industry. A focus on existing customers,
by contrast, tends to drive organizations to
come up with better solutions for them than
what competitors currently offer—but keeps
companies moored in red oceans.

Consider Sony's launch of the Portable Reader System (PRS) in 2006. The company's aim was to unlock a new market space in books by opening the e-reader market to a wide customer base. To figure out how to realize that goal, it looked to the experience of existing e-reader customers, who were dissatisfied with the size and poor display quality of current products. Sony's response was a thin, lightweight device with an easy-to-read screen. Despite the media's praise and happier customers, the PRS lost out to Amazon's Kindle because it failed to attract the mass of noncustomers whose main reason for rejecting e-readers was the shortage of worthwhile books, not the size and the display of the devices. Without a rich choice of titles and an easy way to download them, the noncustomers stuck to print books.

Amazon understood this when it launched the Kindle in 2007, offering more than four times the number of e-titles available from the PRS and making them easily downloadable over Wi-Fi. Within six hours of their release, Kindles sold out, as print book customers rapidly became e-reader customers as well. Though Sony has since exited e-readers, the Kindle grew the industry from around a mere 2% of total book buyers in 2008 to 28% in 2014. It now offers more than 2.5 million e-titles.

TRAP TWO: TREATING MARKET-CREATING STRATEGIES AS NICHE STRATEGIES

The field of marketing has placed great emphasis on using ever finer market segmentation to identify and capture niche markets. Though niche strategies can often be very effective, uncovering a niche in an existing space is not the same thing as identifying a new market space.

Consider Song, an airline launched in 2003 by Delta. Delta's aim was to create a new market space in low-cost carriers by targeting a distinct segment of fliers. It decided to focus on stylish professional women travelers, a segment it figured had needs and preferences different from those of the businessmen and other passengers most airlines targeted. No airline had ever been built around this group. After many focus group discussions with upwardly mobile and professional women, Delta came up with a plan to cater to them with organic food, custom cocktails, a variety of entertainment choices, free in-flight workouts with complementary exercise bands, and crew members dressed in Kate Spade. The strategy was intended to fill a gap in the market. It may well have done that successfully, but the segment proved too small to be sustainable despite competitive pricing. Song flew its last flight in April 2006, just 36 months after its launch.

Successful market-creating strategies don't focus on finer segmentation. More often, they "desegment" markets by identifying key commonalities across buyer groups that could help generate broader demand. Pret A Manger, a British food chain, looked across three different prepared-lunch buyer groups: restaurant-going professionals, fast food customers, and the brown bag set. Although there were plenty of differences across these groups, there were three key commonalities: All of them wanted a lunch that was fresh and healthful, wanted it fast, and wanted it at a reasonable price. That insight helped Pret A Manger see how it could unlock and aggregate untapped demand across those groups to create a commercially compelling new market.

Its concept was to offer restaurant-quality sandwiches made fresh every day from high-end ingredients, preparing them at a speed even greater than that of fast food, and delivering that experience in a sleek setting at reasonable prices. Today, nearly 30 years on, Pret A Manger continues to enjoy robust profitable growth in the new market space it established.

TRAP THREE: CONFUSING TECHNOLOGY INNOVATION WITH MARKET-CREATING STRATEGIES

R&D and technology innovation are widely recognized as key drivers of market development and industry growth. It's understandable, therefore, that managers might assume that they are also key drivers in the discovery of new markets. But the reality is that market creation is not inevitably about technological innovation. Yellow Tail opened a new market (in its case, for a fun and simple wine for everyone) without any bleeding-edge technologies. So did the coffee chain Starbucks and the performing arts company Cirque du Soleil. Even when technology is heavily involved, as it was with market creators Salesforce.com, Intuit's Quicken, or Uber, it is not the reason that new offerings are successful. Such products and services succeed because they are so simple to use, fun, and productive that people fall in love with them. The technology that enables them essentially disappears from buyers' minds.

Consider the Segway Personal Transporter, which was launched in 2001. Was it a technology innovation? Sure. It was the world's first self-balancing human transporter, and it worked well. Lean forward and you go forward; lean back and you go back. This engineering marvel was one of the most-talked-about technology innovations of its time. But most people were unwilling to pay up to $5,000 for a product that posed difficulties in use and convenience: Where could you park it? How would you take it with you in a car? Where could you use it—sidewalks or roads? Could you take it on a bus or a train? Although the Segway was expected to reach breakeven just six months after its launch, sales fell way below initial predictions, and the company was sold in 2009. Not everyone was surprised. At the time of the product's release, a prescient *Time* magazine article about Dean Kamen, Segway's inventor, struck a cautionary note: "One of the hardest truths for any technologist to hear is that success or failure in business is rarely determined by the quality of the technology."

Value innovation, not technology innovation, is what launches commercially compelling new markets. Successful new products or services open market spaces by offering a leap in productivity, simplicity, ease of use, convenience, fun, or environmental friendliness. But when companies mistakenly assume that market creation hinges on breakthrough technologies, their organizations tend to push for products or services that are too "out there," too complicated, or, like the Segway, lacking a necessary ecosystem. In fact, many technology innovations fail to create new markets even if they win the company accolades and their developers scientific prizes.

TRAP FOUR: EQUATING CREATIVE DESTRUCTION WITH MARKET CREATION

Joseph Schumpeter's theory of creative destruction lies at the heart of innovation economics. Creative destruction occurs when an invention disrupts a market by displacing an earlier technology or existing product or service. Digital photography, for example, wiped out the photographic film industry, becoming the new norm. In Schumpeter's framework, the old is incessantly destroyed and replaced by the new.

But does market creation always involve destruction? The answer is no. It also involves nondestructive creation, wherein new demand is created without displacing existing products or services. Take Viagra, which established a new market in lifestyle drugs. Did Viagra make any earlier technology or existing product or service obsolete? No. It unlocked new demand by offering for the first time a real solution to a major problem experienced by many men in their personal relationships. Grameen Bank's creation of the microfinance industry is another example. Many market-creating moves are nondestructive, because they offer solutions where none previously existed. We've also seen this happen with the social networking and crowdfunding industries. And even when a certain amount of destruction is involved in market creation, nondestructive creation is often a larger element than you might think. Nintendo's Wii game player, for example, complemented more than replaced existing game systems, because it attracted younger children and older adults who hadn't previously played video games.

Conflating market creation with creative destruction not only limits an organization's set of opportunities but also sets off resistance to market-creating strategies. People in established companies typically don't like the notion of creative destruction or disruption because it may threaten their current status and jobs. As a result, managers often undermine their company's market-creating efforts by starving them of resources, allocating undue overhead costs to the initiatives, or not cooperating with the people working on them. It's critical for market creators to head this danger off early by clarifying that their project is at least as much about nondestructive creation as it is about disruption.

TRAP FIVE: EQUATING MARKET-CREATING STRATEGIES WITH DIFFERENTIATION

In a competitive industry companies tend to choose their position on what economists call the "productivity frontier," the range of value-cost trade-offs that are available given the structure and norms of the industry. Differentiation is the strategic position on this frontier in which a company stands out from competitors by providing premium value; the trade-off is usually higher costs to the company and higher prices for customers. We've found that many managers assume that market creation is the same thing.

In reality, a market-creating move breaks the value-cost trade-off. It is about pursuing differentiation and low cost simultaneously. Are Yellow Tail and Salesforce.com differentiated from other players? You bet. But are Yellow Tail and Salesforce.com also low cost? Yes again. A market-creating move is a "both-and," not an "either-or," strategy. It's important to realize this difference, because when companies mistakenly assume that market creation is synonymous with differentiation, they often focus on what to improve or create to stand apart and pay scant heed to what they can eliminate or reduce to simultaneously achieve low cost. As a result, they may inadvertently become premium competitors in an existing industry space rather than discover a new market space of their own.

Take BMW, which set out to establish a new market in urban transport with its launch of the C_I in 2000. Traffic problems in European cities are severe, and people waste many hours commuting by car there, so BMW wanted to develop a vehicle people could use to beat rush-hour congestion. The C_I was a two-wheeled scooter targeting the premium end of the market. Unlike other scooters, it had a roof and a full windshield with wipers. BMW also invested heavily in safety. The C_I held drivers in place with a four-point seat-belt system and protected them with an aluminum roll cage, two shoulder-height roll bars, and a crumple zone around the front wheel.

With all these extra features, the C_I was expensive to build, and its price ranged from

$7,000 to $10,000—far more than the $3,000 to $5,000 that typical scooters fetched. Although the C1 succeeded in differentiating itself within the scooter industry, it did not create the new market space in transportation BMW had hoped for. In the summer of 2003, BMW announced it was stopping production because the C1 hadn't met sales expectations.

TRAP SIX: EQUATING MARKET-CREATING STRATEGIES WITH LOW-COST STRATEGIES

This trap, in which managers assume that they can create a new market solely by driving down costs, is the obvious flip side of trap five. When organizations see market-creating strategies as synonymous with low-cost strategies alone, they focus on what to eliminate and reduce in current offerings and largely ignore what they should improve or create to increase the offerings' value.

Ouya is a video-game console maker that fell into this trap. When the company began selling its products, in June 2013, big players like Sony, Microsoft, and Nintendo were offering consoles connected to TV screens and controllers that provided a high-quality gaming experience, for prices ranging from $199 to $419. With no low-cost console available, many people would play video games either on handheld devices or on TV screens connected to mobile devices via inexpensive cables.

An attempt to create a market space between high-end consoles and mobile handhelds, the $99 Ouya was introduced as a low-cost open-source "microconsole" offering reasonable quality on TV screens and most games free to try. Although people admired the inexpensive, simple device, Ouya didn't have the rich catalog of quality games, 3-D intensity, great graphics, and processing speed that traditional gamers prized but the company had to some extent sacrificed to drop cost and price. At the same time, Ouya lacked the distinctive advantage of mobile handheld devices—namely, their play-on-the-go functionality. In the absence of those features, potential gamers had no compelling reason to buy

Ouyas. The company is now shopping itself to acquirers—on the basis of its staff's talent more than the strength of its console business—but as yet hasn't found one.

Our point, again, is that a market-creating strategy takes a "both-and" approach: It pursues both differentiation and low cost. In this framework, new market space is created not by pricing against the competition within an industry but by pricing against substitutes and alternatives that noncustomers are currently using. Accordingly, a new market does not have to be created at the low end of an industry. Instead it can be created at the high end, as Cirque du Soleil did in circus entertainment, Starbucks did in coffee, and Dyson did in vacuum cleaners.

Even when companies create new markets at the low end, the offerings also are clearly differentiated in the eyes of buyers. Consider Southwest Airlines and Swatch. Southwest stands out for its friendly, fast, ground-transportation-in-the-air feel, while stylish, fun designs make Swatches a fashion statement. Both companies' offerings are perceived as both differentiated and low cost.

The approaches or strategies presented as the red ocean traps are not wrong or bad. They all serve important purposes. A customer focus, for example, can improve products and services, and technology innovation is a key input for market development and economic growth. Likewise, differentiation or low cost is an effective competitive strategy. What these approaches are not, however, is the path to successful market-creating strategies. And when they drive market-creating efforts that involve big investments, they may result in new businesses that don't earn back those investments and that ultimately fail, as we have seen here. That's why it's key to surface and check the mental models and assumptions of the people who are central to executing market-creating strategies. If those models and assumptions are misaligned with the intended strategic purpose of new market creation, you need to challenge, question, and reframe them. Otherwise, you may fall into the red ocean traps.

ABOUT THE AUTHORS

W. Chan Kim and *Renée Mauborgne* are professors at INSEAD, the world's second-largest business school, and codirectors of the INSEAD Blue Ocean Strategy Institute. They are the authors of *Blue Ocean Strategy*, which is recognized as one of the most iconic and impactful strategy books ever written. The theory of blue ocean strategy has been actively embraced by companies, governments, and nonprofits across the globe and is currently being taught in more than eighteen hundred universities around the world. *Blue Ocean Strategy* is a bestseller across five continents. It has sold over 3.6 million copies and has been published in a record-breaking 44 languages. Kim and Mauborgne are ranked in the top three of the Thinkers50 global list of top management thinkers and were named among the world's top five best business school professors by MBA Rankings. They have received numerous academic and management awards around the globe, including the Nobels Colloquia Prize for Leadership on Business and Economic Thinking, the Carl S. Sloane Award by the Association of Management Consulting Firms, the Leadership Hall of Fame by *Fast Company* magazine, and the

Eldridge Haynes Prize by the Academy of International Business, among others. Kim and Mauborgne are Fellows of the World Economic Forum in Davos. Mauborgne is a member of President Barack Obama's Board of Advisors on Historically Black Colleges and Universities (HBCUs). Kim is an advisory member for the European Union and is an advisor for several countries.

ALSO BY THESE AUTHORS

Harvard Business Review Press Books

*Blue Ocean Strategy, Expanded Edition:
How to Create Uncontested Market Space
and Make the Competition Irrelevant*

*The W. Chan Kim and Renée Mauborgne
Blue Ocean Strategy Reader*

Harvard Business Review Articles

"Blue Ocean Leadership"

"Blue Ocean Strategy"

"Charting Your Company's Future"

"Creating New Market Space"

"Fair Process: Managing in the Knowledge Economy"

"How Strategy Shapes Structure"

"Knowing a Winning Business Idea When You See One"

"Tipping Point Leadership"

"Value Innovation: The Strategic Logic of High Growth"

Article Summary

Idea in Brief

The Problem

To succeed in the long term, companies must find ways to create new markets. Competing in existing markets is growing less profitable. But despite much investment and commitment, companies find it extraordinarily difficult to establish new market spaces.

Why It Happens
Managers' mental models are based on their experiences in existing markets. Though these assumptions and beliefs have worked in the past, they undermine efforts to create new spaces.

The Solution
To avoid being trapped in old markets, managers need to:

- focus on attracting new customers

- worry less about segmentation

- understand that market creation is not synonymous with either technological innovation or creative destruction

- stop focusing on premium versus low-cost strategies

CREATE UNCONTESTED MARKET SPACE AND MAKE THE COMPETITION IRRELEVANT

If you enjoyed reading *Blue Ocean Leadership*, turn to this expanded edition of the landmark bestseller *Blue Ocean Strategy*, embraced by business leaders and organizations worldwide.

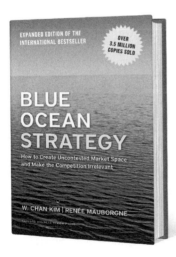

hbr.org/books

Invaluable insights
always at your fingertips

With an All-Access subscription to *Harvard Business Review*, you'll get so much more than a magazine.

Exclusive online content and tools
you can put to use today

My Library, your personal workspace for sharing, saving, and organizing HBR.org articles and tools

---

Unlimited access to more than 4,000 articles in the *Harvard Business Review* archive

---

Subscribe today at hbr.org/subnow

The most important management ideas all in one place.

We hope you enjoyed this book from *Harvard Business Review*. For the best ideas HBR has to offer turn to HBR's 10 Must Reads Boxed Set. From books on leadership and strategy to managing yourself and others, this 6-book collection delivers articles on the most essential business topics to help you succeed.

HBR's 10 Must Reads Series

The definitive collection of ideas and best practices on our most sought-after topics from the best minds in business.

- Change Management
- Collaboration
- Communication
- Emotional Intelligence
- Innovation
- Leadership
- Making Smart Decisions
- Managing Across Cultures
- Managing People
- Managing Yourself
- Strategic Marketing
- Strategy
- Teams
- The Essentials

hbr.org/mustreads

Buy for your team, clients, or event.
Visit hbr.org/bulksales for quantity discount rates.